THIS BOOK BELONGS TO
The Library of

....

....

Did you like my book? I pondered it severely before releasing this book. Although the response has been overwhelming, it is always pleasing to see, read or hear a new comment. Thank you for reading this and I would love to hear your honest opinion about it. Furthermore, many people are searching for a unique book, and your feedback will help me gather the right books for my reading audience.

Thanks!

Table of Contents

Introduction

Congratulations on purchasing *This Book,* and thank you for doing so! You're finally taking the first step in taking charge of your life, your finances, your future, your money, and creating your own business.

There are so many people in the world who dream of being successful, who talk to anyone and everyone who will listen about what they would do if they could own their own business, and how they would live their dream life if only they had the money to do it. These are what I call "if I only won the lottery" people, because most of their talk revolves around them winning the lottery or coming into a large, substantial inheritance, and how they would change their lives with their sudden windfall.

You know someone like this. You have heard them talk about their plans, you have listened to countless conversations about their dreams, what they would do if they had the money and the opportunity, and how different their life would be "if only I won the lottery."

These people will never realize their Dream Life, will never reach their goals, and will always live the exact way they are living right now because they refuse to do what you have already started to do: they are not taking control of their life and their finances. They are not working towards their goals and making their Dream Life a reality. You are.

By purchasing *This Book* and following the lessons and information I have presented in it, you are taking ownership of your life, leaving the dream state of "if I only won the lottery," and living in a reality where you are in control, where you are in charge, and where you will be successful. Now that you have the tools that you need, it is up to you to adopt a winning attitude and provide yourself with the life you desire and deserve.

We have all heard the old adage that "time is money" and, while that may be true, it is not the entire story. Saying that "time is money" is similar to saying that you have "no time to lose," and that is much closer to the truth. You have no time to lose and need to begin working towards your dreams and your goals right now. In another sense, no matter where you are in life, it is never too late to work towards your dreams. By taking the first step in purchasing this book, you have already started on the journey towards making your goals become a reality and creating the Dream Life that you have always wanted.

You should never exchange time for money because, while you can always make more money, you cannot make more time. Time is of a finite quantity, and, as such, you should guard it just as carefully as you guard your money, maybe more so, since so many people squander both their money and their time carelessly.

Think of yourself as having two incomes: money and time. Both can be spent on things that you want. Money can buy clothes, a house, opportunities to have experiences, and much, much more. Time can buy moments with your family, moments creating experiences that you will never forget, and time spent doing activities and things that you want to do.

When you begin separating time and money, you can begin to see what you spend each of your incomes on. Are you spending your money on things that are meaningless and will not get you the Dream Life you want, that will not help you to achieve the goals you have in mind for yourself and your life? Are you spending time helping other people achieve their dreams, but leaving your own unfulfilled and languishing? Once you begin to detach money from time, you change the equation as well as your life's balance.

In order to live the Dream Life you want, you cannot depend on others to help you do it. Bosses come and go. Employees come and go. Even jobs will come and go. The stock market will go up. The stock market will go down. Our world is a constantly changing, constantly moving, constantly evolving, living, breathing organism where the only three certainties are:

1. You have a limited amount of time every day (twenty-four hours) and only so many days in your entire life.

2. Time is the most valuable asset you have in your life.

3. You are the only person that you can truly depend upon to help you achieve the goals and desires that you have.

Time is such an important commodity, and you cannot waste it, let other people be in control of it, or allow others to take it away from you. Just like money, you should be guarding your time and actively choosing what you are spending your time upon. If you let somebody else be in control of your time, you are giving them control over you, over your life, over your goals, over your future, and you are working on making ***somebody else's*** Dream Life come true.

The simple fact is that in order to live the life that you have always wanted to live, your Dream Life, you cannot depend on others. You need to create your own source of income, and you need to create something that generates money non stop, twenty-four hours a day, and three hundred sixty-five days a year. You need to stop allowing people to take away, or steal, your time, just like you would stop people from taking away, or stealing, your money. Time is the most valuable asset you have, and it is time that you start treating it as such.

Right now, you are at Point A. Point A is the place where:

· you do not know what to do in life

· you may have ideas, but they are scattered

· you do not have a plan

· you are not living the life that you want to live

· other people are in control of your time, money, and your life

Our goal, in following the steps and advice this book, is to get you to Point B. Point B is the place where:

· you know exactly what to do in life and in business

· you have concrete, grounded ideas

- you have a solid, fully formed plan

- you are living the Dream Life that you have always wanted

- you are in complete control of your time, your money, your goals, and your Dream Life

This book has been divided into two Parts. Part One is the **Right Mindset**. In Part One, we will look at you and your life. What is your Dream Life and why are you not already living it? What is keeping you from achieving your dreams and preventing you from living your Dream Life? What are the parts of your life that make you happy and are worth your time? What areas of your life need more focus, what areas of your life need change, and what areas of your life need cutting away because they are holding you and your success back?

We will answer all of these questions and more in Part One: Right Mindset, where you will create goals, identify what it is that you want out of life, articulate what your Dream Life looks like, and begin to format a plan for owning your own business.

Part Two is the **Repeatable Path**. Making money does not work if it is only a one time deal. There is a reason why most people who come into a large sum of money all at once, such as an inheritance or winning the lottery, are broke again within five years. Getting a single paycheck will not sustain you, your goals, and your Dream Life for the rest of your life. You need to make money continuously from now until you die. The more money you make means the less time that you are forced to spend your money and time on things you do not want to, in effect wasting your assets (your time and your money) on things that have no meaning to you.

In Part Two: Repeatable Path, we will look at what it takes to plan, create, and start your own business, what pitfalls and potential road blocks you need to identify and plan for, and how to protect yourself, your business, and your assets from any negative turns the economy or stock market might take, from anyone who wants a piece of your hard work and Dream Life, and from other threats to you, your goals, and your Dream Life. You will also build your own business in Part Two, taking it from ideas to opportunities to a solid Business Plan.

Part 1: Right Mindset

In order to achieve any sort of greatness in life, in order to reach your goals and to live your Dream Life, you need the Right Mindset.

What is the Right Mindset? The Right Mindset is how Winners think. The Right Mindset is how anyone who has achieved their dreams and is living their Dream Life thinks. The Right Mindset is what separates those who have achieved their goals and are living their Drem Life from those who are still working for others, wishing that their lives were different.

What is the difference between you and them? You are about to find out.

Go stand in front of a mirror. Right now. Do not keep reading this book and not do what I am telling you to do. Remember, you are changing your life, and that means you need to take action, not sit around and expect everything to just happen on its own. Why would you hesitate to do this? Do you feel embarrassed or uncertain? Do not. Take a deep breath, let it out, and remind yourself that you are about to change your life and that this is the first step.

Take this book, go to the nearest mirror, and stand in front of it. Are you there? Can you see yourself? Good. Now, look at yourself. Start with the top of your head and slowly work your way down as far as you can see in the mirror. Starting at the bottom, go back up, looking at every part of you along the way. When you reach the top of your head, do it again.

Look into your eyes. When you look at yourself, and when you look into your eyes, what do you see? Do you see a Winner? Do you see someone in charge of their life? Do you see someone with all of the right answers? Do you see someone who has made the right choices and is living the life that they have always wanted to live?

No? Then what _do_ you really see? Do you see someone who needs to lose weight? Do you see someone who dresses like a slob? Do you see someone who is slouched down, not standing up straight, and who looks like they do not know what they want out of life? Do you see someone who is overwhelmed with problems and looking for answers? Do you see someone who once had dreams, thought that they knew where they were going, but time seems to have gotten away from them, and now they are living a life that is very, very different than the one that they had envisioned five or ten years ago? Do you see someone who lets others control their decisions, their choices, and their life? It is also important to make these goals something attainable and positive. You will not feel like a winner if you are knocking yourself for something that you can't change. Though physical appearance can be changed, a large part of being successful is becoming confident with what the best version of you is.

If you look into the mirror and do not see a Winner, you need to change that perception and change how you look at yourself. This is the first and the most important step in changing your life, building your own business, and creating the Dream Life that you want.

Take this book and go get something to write with (pencil, pen, et cetera) and either sticky notes, paper, or use your computer and printer.

Ready? Now, think back to what you saw in the mirror. What are things about yourself (physically, emotionally, and mentally) that you would like to change? Make a list of them, in no particular order, on your paper. When you write each item down, be descriptive and direct, and make it an "I want" statement. Now is not the time for making things sound better than they are, but for the absolute, unvarnished truth.

For example:

- I want to be more authoritative when I speak and not sound so timid.

- I want to lose 35 pounds.

- I want to be able to climb stairs without being winded and having to take a break halfway up.

- I want to be able to talk to strangers while looking them in the eye instead of always looking at the ground.

- I want to be able to talk to a room full of people without stuttering and blushing.

- I want to look "neat" and not "messy," or like I just got out of bed.

- I want people to listen when I speak and not engage in side conversations because I am not dynamic enough to hold their attention.

- I want to dress like an adult instead of continuing to wear the same clothes I wore in high school.

- I want to be "tougher" and not cry every time someone says something negative to me.

- I want to stop living with my parents (or roommates) and be on my own.

YOU ARE A WINNER. You need to act like a Winner every moment of the day, so that not only will you believe it, but others will believe it, too. You need to be a Winner first with yourself, with how you see yourself, then with others. This attitude and personae are critical and will take work. A Winner is a Winner every moment of every day, not just sometimes or occasionally. Even when no one is around, you are still a Winner and must always believe it, say it, show it, and act like it. Being a Winner is not a costume you put on and take off; it is who you really are all of the time.

CHAPTER 1

Looking Like a Winner

Do you look like a Winner? From your personal appearance to your clothes, how do you see yourself, and how do others see you as well?

Begin by looking closely at your appearance. Winners dress like Winners. They dress like the professionals that they are. They do not wear pajamas except to bed, and they never wear them in public. They do not wear clothing that is dirty, wrinkled, stained, or torn. They wear clothes that fit without being too tight or too baggy. They were clothing that is appropriate, meaning professional and not too revealing, too young, or what could better be described as a costume. Winners do not have to dress with the latest fashions, because most Winners wear clothing that is timeless.

Do you dress like a Winner, like the Winner that you want to be? Do you dress like the professional that you want to be? If you do not, you need to begin right now. No one will take you seriously, and you cannot take yourself seriously, if you do not look the part of a professional and if you do not look like a Winner.

No matter what you are doing, whether it is working out at the gym, going to the grocery store to buy groceries, taking the dog to the park for a walk, or meeting a few friends after work for cocktails, you should always look like a Winner. This starts with how you are dressed and what you wear every moment of the day.

You do not have to spend a lot of money to dress like a Winner, either. If you live near a resale shop or thrift store, you can easily find discounted, name brand clothing that makes you look professional. One of the best investments you can make is to have a jacket or dress tailored for yourself. A person that does alterations or tailor will normally charge a few dollars to hem a pair of pants or properly cuff a shirt and the change in your outfit's appearance and in how people see you is well worth the nominal investment.

Are you clueless when it comes to how to dress or what style you should be wearing? Any department store, clothing store, or clothing boutique will have knowledgeable sales people who can help you determine what best fits your body and your style. You do not have to commit to purchasing the clothes from them, although you can if you so choose. You should visit with more than one person and learn what you can from each: what looks best on you, what styles work best, et cetera.

What about the rest of your appearance? What about you yourself? When you look in the mirror, are you well groomed? Is your hair styled every day? Or are you overdue for a haircut? Have you had the same hairstyle since middle school? Do you need to lose weight? Do you slouch when you sit or walk? Do you duck your head down instead of looking straight ahead and meeting people in the eye? Do you bite your nails? Be honest and critical about your appearance, because that is the first thing everyone will see when they meet you. Would you trust yourself with an investment? With a product? With someone else's money? With some else's Dream Life?

Mark Wahlberg is one of the most famous actors in the world, an entrepreneur, husband, family man, son, devout Catholic, and . . . well, the list goes on and on. This is a person who anyone would think was nearly perfect and has the absolute Dream Life. What separates him from you?

Mark Wahlberg did not obtain his success in life because of luck. He did not become who he is because someone gave him a break, a leg up, or his big chance. He has not attained the status that he currently occupies in life because of anything other than hard work, honesty, and dedication. When he was younger and lived a life where he regularly broke the law, he looked in the mirror one day and decided that he wanted to change, that he was unhappy with who he was. Mark Wahlberg wanted to have his Dream Life, and he took a long, hard look at himself in the mirror, asking himself tough questions along the way. Was he someone that others would look up to? Was he someone that others would take seriously? Was he proud of himself and the choices that he was making? Was he a success?

No, he was not. He did not like who he was, he did not like how he was living his life, and he decided to change it. Knowing that no one was going to do it for him, he knew that he would have to do all of the hard work on his own.

Mark Wahlberg wakes up at 2:30 every morning and dedicates the first several hours of his day to improving himself: spiritually, physically, emotionally, and in his relationships. He wakes up so early because he works on himself **before** he begins his day interacting with other people, before he begins his job, before he allows others to see him as the successful, professional person he has become.

You need to develop the same focus, intensity, and passion when you look at yourself in the mirror. When you look in a mirror, and the first thing you think is "Winner," then when others see you, that will be the first thing they think of as well.

CHAPTER 2

Feeling Like a Winner

Do you feel like a Winner? Inside and outside, when you think about yourself, do you <u>really</u> feel like a Winner?

You have been doing really well, and we have covered a lot of information already. Right now, it is time for a break (and for our next activity). Take this book and get something to write with (pencil, pen, et cetera) and either sticky notes, paper and tape, or use your computer and printer. Also, gather the list that you made earlier with the things about yourself that you want to change.

Do you have everything ready? If so, you need to look back in the same mirror you just used and identify three things about yourself that you want to change. They do not all have to be huge or dramatic changes. It is okay to begin with one big change and a couple of smaller changes. Use the list of things you have already created and, looking in the mirror, identify the three that are the most important to you.

On three separate pieces of paper, write affirmations about being a Winner that mark the changes you will be making. Write them as positive statements that turn what you want to change into a reason why you are changing that trait about yourself.

For example:

- WINNERS stand up straight, tall, and proud, and they look people in the eye when they speak.

- WINNERS are well groomed and never leave the bathroom without looking "put together", even if they are alone in their apartment.

- WINNERS care about themselves and their health. They take care of their bodies just like they take care of their money and their time.

- WINNERS dress like the successful professionals that they are because they are always ready to make a phenomenal first impression.

- WINNERS speak directly, clearly, and with confidence because they know what they are talking about and have confidence in what they are saying.

Write the three affirmations that you created out again on three more sets of paper, for a total of twelve sheets. (The three sheets you created first, then three copies of each affirmation.) Place one set of affirmations next to your bed, so that the first thing you see in the morning and the last thing you see at night are your statements about being a winner. Place one set of affirmations in your dressing area or bathroom, so that when you stare in the mirror, you are repeating the words to yourself over and over again. Place the third set of affirmations on the back of your door, so that the last thing you see when you leave your house every day are your Winner affirmations.

Place the last set of affirmations in your carry all, brief case, purse, date book, laptop bag, or whatever you carry with you in your day to day travels. During the day, when you feel yourself slipping back into the wrong mindset, take the Winner affirmation papers out and repeat them to yourself, over and over, until you get back on track and back into the Right Mindset.

Remember, no one will believe you are a Winner unless you believe it about yourself first. You need to start seeing that you are a Winner in everything you say and do and you need to treat yourself like the Winner that you are. No more shortcuts to staying fit and healthy. No more lazy days where you stay in your pajamas all day. No more missed or skipped appointments at the barber or the salon because "it really is not all *that* bad". Yes, it is, and you, a Winner, can do better. You <u>deserve</u> better.

CHAPTER 3

What is Your Dream Life?

You can achieve your Dream Life. You can live the way you have always wanted to live. You can accomplish your goals and be the success that you have always imagined yourself to be.

Now, the next step in achieving the Right Mindset is to look at your Dream Life and articulate exactly what it is that you want. First, this needs to be an honest conversation with yourself, where you reflect on authentic goals, realistic objectives, and attainable dreams.

This is not a book that is selling you a "pie in the sky" optimism where "everyone is a winner" and "everyone gets a trophy and ice cream with sprinkles". No, not everyone can be President. No, not everyone can be an astronaut. No, not everyone can marry J-Lo. Anyone who has ever told you that you can be anything you want to in life has lied to you. I am not going to lie to you. I did not write this book and share with you my own strategies and successes in order to tell you anything but the absolute truth. Your dreams need to be realistic and, honestly, the first one should be for "happy" or "happiness".

It is not going to do you any good to achieve your Dream Life if you are miserable while you do it, or after you have it. No one pictures their future, pictures living their Dream Life, and sees themselves as miserable. What would make you the most happy in life?

For example:

- Do you want to own your own home with no mortgage looming over you for the next fifteen to thirty years?

- Do you want to travel around the country or around the world?

- Do you want to start a scholarship to honor the memory of a relative or friend?

- Do you want to have time every week to volunteer at your local animal shelter?

- Do you want to buy and design a community garden and grow your own vegetables and fruits with your neighbors?

- Do you want to get married and have a family?

- Do you want to ensure that your parents are taken care of after they retire and not worry about them struggling to pay their bills, afford medication, and buy food?

- Do you want to be debt free and have financial security for the rest of your life?

Take a moment and think about what would make you the happiest in life. What does your Dream Life look like? Take this book and get something to write with (pencil, pen, et cetera) and either sticky notes, paper and tape, or use your computer and printer.

Do you have everything ready? If not, then please do not read any further until you do. Remember, you are working on having the Right Mindset and being a Winner. You cannot do that until you are ready.

If so, you need to think back to the Dream Life that you just envisioned. Write down what your Dream Life looks like using a positive, goal setting statement on a single sheet of paper or a sticky note.

For example:

- To achieve my DREAM LIFE goals of being debt free, owning a home, having a family, and having the time to volunteer with at risk youth from my neighborhood, I will keep my eyes focused on the future, remember that I am a WINNER, and make only the choices that will lead to my DREAM LIFE.

- I will reach my DREAM LIFE and achieve a comfortable retirement lifestyle, travel the world with my husband, and have time to paint by making the choices of a WINNER: be professional, be dedicated, control my own time, and control my own money.

- My DREAM LIFE sees me living near the ocean in a beach house where I have time for surfing, cookouts on the beach with my friends, and deep sea fishing and I will achieve this through being a WINNER, owning my own business, and controlling all of my assets myself (time and money).

Place your Dream Life goal next to where you spend the most time in the morning, like on the easel of your stair climbing machine because you begin each day with a workout, on the kitchen table where you sit to have coffee and read every morning, or on the mirror of the bathroom because you spend thirty minutes grooming every morning.

Every morning read your Dream Life goal out loud to yourself and picture what that Dream Life will look like, what it will smell like, what it will taste like, and what it will feel like, until you can visualize every aspect of your Dream Life and it is as real to you now as it will be when you finally achieve it.

CHAPTER 4

Work for it

You are worth the work. You are worth the effort. You are worth the time, the energy, and the toil that it will take you and all of the steps that you will have to do in order to achieve your goals and live your Dream Life.

This is a critical step for you: Do not take short cuts on any of the steps that we have implemented so far. I will repeat: *do not take short cuts on any of the steps that we have implemented so far.* It is <u>essential</u> that you daily reaffirm your place as a Winner and your goals for your Dream Life. Every day you must work on having the Right Mindset and thinking, and acting, like a Winner. You cannot have success in your outside life if you do not have success in your inside life.

That is to say, if you are not a Winner on the inside, you will not be one on the outside. Being a Winner starts from within.

Achieving your Dream Life, having all of the time you want and the ability to spend that time on the things that you choose to spend it on, and being in control of all areas of your life (money, time, responsibilities, et cetera) is not easy and it is not something that happens automatically. Let us be honest with one another. If any of these things were easy, everyone would be doing them, everyone would be living their Dream Life, and everyone would be in charge of their own lives.

Achieving your Dream Life is not, however, like winning the lottery. That is a matter of luck, and only one person out of hundreds of millions of people will have that one winning ticket. You do not need luck to achieve and live your Dream Life. You can achieve your Dream Life by following the steps in this book, including those critical daily Winner affirmations that you have placed all around you, as well as by forming a plan and by working to reach your goals.

Part of your daily schedule will include working on yourself, on being the Winner that you are, and on working on your Dream Life. Why is a schedule so important? Keep reading, and you will see why Winners have schedules that they stick to, even on the weekends.

CHAPTER 5

Having Discipline

Winners are not spontaneous; they stick to lists and a schedule because order and discipline are two characteristics of every Winner who has ever lived, throughout history.

Two traits that link all Winners and people of wealth is that they have a schedule that they keep to, day after day, no matter what, and they also make and check off lists.

That is the next step in your path towards becoming the Winner that you are and showing that to the world. What is your current schedule? Do you keep to your schedule, day after day, even on the weekends? Doing so shows your discipline and dedication to yourself and to being the Winner that you are. Part of having the Right Mindset is the discipline to adhere to a schedule.

Take a few minutes and think about what you do on a daily basis. Take this book and get something to write with (pencil, pen, et cetera) and either sticky notes, paper and tape, or use your computer and printer. Write out your schedule from the time you wake up to the time that you go to sleep. Account for every minute of your day and be specific in naming what you are doing.

For example:

6:30 wake up and have coffee

7:00 eat breakfast and read the paper

7:45 shower, shave and get dressed

8:15 catch the train for work

8:30 work

12:00 lunch

12:30 work

5:00 catch the train for home

5:15 stop by the deli for dinner ingredients

5:45 cook dinner and eat

6:30 talk to parents in Florida

7:00 watch television

10:00 go to bed

Now, pull out your Winner affirmations from your briefcase or laptop bag or purse. Place them beside your schedule. Look over your schedule critically and ask yourself, where are you actively working on your first Winner affirmation? On your second Winner affirmation? On your third Winner affirmation? Rewrite your schedule to include time in your day to actively work on each Winner affirmation, making sure that you highlight the Winner affirmation in your schedule.

You may need to adjust your schedule to fit everything in. This is one of the times and the exercise where you are actively spending your time in an effort to afford your Dream Life.

For example:

6:00 wake up, say Winner daily affirmations and have coffee, eat breakfast, and read the paper

6:30 exercise (Monday, Wednesday, Friday) and stretch (Tuesday, Thursday)

WINNERS care about themselves and their health. They take care of their bodies just like they take care of their money and their time.

7:15 shower, shave and get dressed, repeating daily Winner affirmations

WINNERS dress like the successful professionals that they are because they are always ready to make a phenomenal first impression.

8:15 catch the train for work, taking an after workout smoothie

8:30 work

WINNERS stand up straight, tall, and proud, and they look people in the eye when they speak.

12:00 lunch

12:30 work

WINNERS stand up straight, tall, and proud, and they look people in the eye when they speak.

5:00 catch the train for home

5:15 stop by the deli for dinner ingredients

5:45 cook dinner and eat

6:30 talk to parents in Florida

7:00 watch news

7:30 watch television

9:00 prepare after workout smoothie for tomorrow, iron clothes for tomorrow, and shine shoes

9:30 go to bed, saying daily Winner affirmations beforehand

Notice the differences? The first schedule looked complete but, when you place the two schedules side by side and compare the first schedule to the second schedule, you see that there were quite a few things missing, all of them to do with being a Winner. I took thirty minutes from the end of the day and moved it to the beginning in order to have more time before work to exercise. Since I did not want to interrupt my sleep, I took the same amount of time out of watching television to replace the sleep, so the schedule changes did not actually cost me any time. (I could have "spent" some of my time to "pay" for the changes, of course, but there was no need.)

Now, think about the tasks that you both want and need to do every day, or every week, and write them down in a list. These may be errands, tasks, chores, hobbies, or other items to be checked off your list.

For example:

- answer e-mails

- grocery shop

- wash dishes

- put dishes away

- clean house

- laundry

- meet friends for social hour

- read

- listen to music

- take suits to the dry cleaner

- pay bills

- shop for elderly neighbor's groceries

- visit library

Most people use the weekends to take care of all of these items. You will now write out a weekend schedule, but do not try to fit all of these items into it. Instead, make sure that you have a balance of work and play every day of the week. Go back to your weekday schedule and modify it as needed so that, when you look at your weekend schedule and your weekday schedule, you have every item on your list accounted for and scheduled for.

CHAPTER 6

Keeping a Schedule

Remember that your time is the most important asset you have, and you need to spend it wisely <u>every</u> day of the week, including the weekends.

For example (weekday schedule):

6:00 wake up, say Winner daily affirmations and have coffee, eat breakfast, and read the paper

6:30 exercise (Monday, Wednesday, Friday) and stretch (Tuesday, Thursday)

WINNERS care about themselves and their health. They take care of their bodies just like they take care of their money and their time.

7:15 shower, shave and get dressed, repeating daily Winner affirmations

WINNERS dress like the successful professionals that they are because they are always ready to make a phenomenal first impression.

8:15 catch the train for work, taking an after workout smoothie

8:30 work

WINNERS stand up straight, tall, and proud, and they look people in the eye when they speak.

12:00 lunch

12:30 work

WINNERS stand up straight, tall, and proud and they look people in the eye when they speak.

5:00 catch the train for home

5:15 pick up mail for the neighbor and say hello

5:45 cook dinner and eat

6:30 talk to parents in Florida

7:00 watch news

7:30 answer email, watch television and read

9:00 prepare after workout smoothie for tomorrow, iron clothes for tomorrow, and shine shoes

9:30 go to bed, saying daily Winner affirmations beforehand

For example (weekend schedule):

6:00 wake up, say Winner daily affirmations and have coffee, eat breakfast, and read the paper

6:30 exercise (Sunday) and stretch (Saturday)

WINNERS care about themselves and their health. They take care of their bodies just like they take care of their money and their time.

7:15 shower, shave and get dressed, repeating daily Winner affirmations

WINNERS dress like the successful professionals that they are because they are always ready to make a phenomenal first impression.

8:15 stop by the neighbor's for their grocery list and say hello

8:30 shop for groceries (Saturday) or listen to music (Sunday)

WINNERS care about themselves and their health. They take care of their bodies just like they take care of their money and their time.

10:00 put groceries away, clean, and do laundry

12:00 meet friends for lunch

WINNERS stand up straight, tall, and proud, and they look people in the eye when they speak.

2:00 go to the library and return books (Saturday) or volunteer   (Sunday)

3:30 pay bills, answer e-mail, run errands (Saturday) and paint   (Sunday)

5:30 cook dinner and eat

6:30 talk to parents in Florida

7:00 watch news

7:30 answer email, watch television and read

9:00 prepare after workout smoothie for tomorrow, iron clothes   for tomorrow, and shine shoes

9:30 go to bed, saying daily Winner affirmations beforehand

CHAPTER 7

Attitude is Everything

Being a Winner is all about being a hard worker, not for others but for yourself, and realizing that you are worth the work. Get into the Right Mindset and stay there.

To be a Winner, you do not need to be especially gifted or even particularly smart. You simply need to do the right things the right way at the right time. If I were to bet, I would say that you have heard the phrase "work sucks" at least once in your life, but probably a lot more often than that. What you have not heard is, "winning sucks," have you? Why is there a difference between the two?

People who have difficulty with work and working are usually either working in a capacity that does not challenge them, does not meet their needs, or does not make them happy. These are people who are spending their time working for others, not for themselves. If you spend all of your time helping someone else to be successful, helping someone else to reach their goals and helping someone else to achieve their Dream Life, then you will begin to resent the job that you are doing, the work that you are doing, and the person that you are doing it for.

When you are working towards achieving your own Dream Life, spending your time helping yourself improve yourself and reach your goals, focusing on making yourself successful, happy, and productive, the work is not tedious, it is not drudgery, and it does not "suck." Work is not a problem. It is what and who you are working for that is the problem. When you are not working towards reaching your own goals, helping your own business advance, and creating your own Dream Life, that is when you begin to resent the work that you are doing.

You may have to keep working in your current job until you have everything ready to pursue your Dream Life. Do not think of this job as a "waste of time" or "tedious" because by continuing to work at it, it is allowing you the time and the money to work towards your Dream Life. Whatever job you are currently doing, whether you are a Day Care Teacher with a room full of four year olds or a Ticket Taker on a subway stop who works the graveyard shift or a substitute Receptionist in the front office of a company, use that job to practice and hone your Winner attitude and self.

Look at your Winner affirmations. How could you work towards accomplishing these goals while still working at your current job? Could you walk around more to increase your level of physical activity in order to help you lose weight? Could you use the opportunities to interact with customers or clients to practice your assertiveness and straightforward attitude?

Every person you see and meet every day is an opportunity to practice greeting others with confidence and self assurance. Every interaction you have with another at work has the possibility to become a way for you to reach one of your goals of being a Winner. Did you look them in the eye? Was your handshake firm and straight forward without being weak or crushing? Did you say hello is a confident manner without stuttering or becoming flustered?

Use your time interacting with others, from people on the subway to the clerk at the grocery store and from your daily coworkers to the barista at the coffee shop, to work on projecting the attitude of a Winner until it is natural, effortless, and a true part of who you are. If you think like a Winner, look like a Winner, speak like a Winner, and feel like a Winner, then you truly **are a Winner**.

CHAPTER 8

Your Surroundings

Do your surroundings say "Winner" to yourself and others?
Do you see a "Winner" when you look around you right now?

When you read these questions, did you immediately think about living in a large home or mansion, complete with manicured lawns, topiaries flanking the front door, and some well regimented gardens separated by footpaths in the back? That is not what I meant at all.

Look around your home right now. Does it say "Winner" to you? Is the bed made? Are the dishes clean and put away? Have you dusted this week? (Or even this month?) Do the windows sparkle because they are clean? Are there cobwebs in the corners of the ceiling? What does your work area look like?

Being a Winner does not stop with making sure _you_ look and act like a Winner twenty-four hours a day, seven days a week. It also means making sure that your surroundings look like those of a

Winner. You have not spent all of the time and effort that you have to create the Right Mindset to just ignore your surroundings. A Winner deserves to have a home that reflects your Right Mindset and reflects the care and attention that you have given to yourself.

Making your bed every day is not about following any dictates leftover from childhood. It is about discipline, routine, and order. Washing the dishes after every meal, even if you only dirtied a fork and a plate, is about projecting the personae and attitude of a Winner. Winners do not live in filth, dirt, and grime, with dirty clothes on the floor, dirty dishes in the kitchen sink, and mail scattered on the countertop.

When anyone walks into your home, no matter how modest or grand it is, that home should be neat, uncluttered, and clean. After all, it is a representation of you, the Winner, and how you conduct yourself at all times, not just when others are watching. Part of your daily schedule should include cleaning, even if it is only for five or ten minutes. Rotate chores each day so that one day you dust, another day you sweep or vacuum, another day you clean the windows, and so forth.

Taking the time to ensure that your home looks like that of a Winner is what you should expect from yourself. After all, you are a Winner, and your home should reflect that. Nothing is too much trouble for you, because you deserve a place that represents who you are, and that begins with having an organized, clean, and uncluttered home.

The same goes for your vehicle and your workplace. Do you routinely clean your vehicle? Or do you throw trash on the floorboards because you are the only person who sees it? It does not take very long (about five minutes) to keep a car clean, dusted, and vacuumed, but the impression you make with a clean vehicle is one that is worth far more than the time you put into it.

Look at the outside of your car. When was the last time you washed it? When was the last time you cleaned the glass and mirrors, both inside and out? Your car does not have to be the newest model in order to project the image of a Winner; it just has to be clean, both inside and out, without layers of dust or grime marring the paint and the rims.

When you go to work, do you have a space that is all your own? Even if it is just a single employee locker, is it neat, clean, and orderly? These things matter, because they say a lot about you, the Winner, and people will judge you on every aspect of your life, from how neat and uncluttered your desk is to if your tie is stain free or if your car is clean when you unexpectedly have to carpool the boss to a meeting in another location because his or her car is being serviced that day. Always be prepared for others to see all areas of your life and to judge those areas. Always surround yourself with the environment of a Winner, because that is what you are. Show it to yourself and to the world.

CHAPTER 9

How to Speak Like a Winner

Do you talk and think like a Winner? When you hear yourself inside your head, or when you speak out loud, do your words sound like those of a Winner?

There are two words that, if you are not paying careful attention, can look the same: winner and whiner. Whiners. We all know of at least one of them. These are the people that are the first to complain about everything: work, about last minute meetings that everyone has to scramble to prepare for, family, friends, their car breaking down over and over. You name it and this person could, and often does, complain about it. This is the kind of person that would complain about receiving an unexpected bonus at work because now they have to pay taxes on it, or being invited to have dinner with the Prime Minister, because that means they now have to go buy a new outfit to wear. Whiners are people who complain about any (and every) thing and manage to turn any good news into a negative diatribe.

Winners, on the other hand, are those people who rise to the challenge and the occasion every time. Is work at the company not going well and there have been talks about reductions or even eliminations? Fantastic, they have several ideas on how to improve efficiency and save the company money while still keeping the same staff levels. There is a last minute meeting in twenty minutes, and everyone should bring their latest earnings report? No problem and they even have projections ready for the next quarter, just in case they are needed.

Winners are not whiners. When faced with a problem, they always have several solutions to it. When you go to someone at work or in your personal life with a problem, are you taking them the problem, expecting them to fix it? Are you just whining about it? Or do you go to them with a problem as well as solutions on how it can be addressed and fixed?

When life takes a turn for the worse, and something breaks or goes wrong, what is your first reaction? Whine about it? Or do you treat it as an opportunity? Do you have back up plans and strategies for when things do not go your way or when problems arise? Winners do.

Let us do an exercise in being a Winner. Take this book and get something to write with (pencil, pen, et cetera) and either sticky notes, some paper, or use your computer and printer. Read each scenario, one at a time, write it out on your paper, and respond to the question using what you would actually do if this were to happen to you. If this has actually happened to you before, write down how you actually responded in that situation in the past.

Scenario A

Your boss comes to you at 4:30 on Friday, when the office is scheduled to close at 4:45 and tells you that you need to finish writing a report for another colleague who had to go home early. You know that this will take at least an hour. How do you respond?

Scenario B

Your car breaks down for the fifth time in four months. You have already spent over two thousand dollars at the repair shop and have been late to work several times because of it. What do you do?

Scenario C

Your brother calls you and says that he was fired (again) from his job and asks if he can come crash at your place, just until he gets back on his feet. The last three times he did this, it was always for at least a month, and he never cleaned, never helped with bills or groceries, and left his laundry for you to do. What do you tell him?

Each of these scenarios are common occurrences that have probably happened to you, or someone you know well, in the past. Look at your responses to each scenario. Did you respond like a Winner or a whiner? In your response, did you take charge or let others dictate to you?

Let us look at these responses to the three scenarios.

Scenario A

Your boss comes to you at 4:30 on Friday, when the office is scheduled to close at 4:45, and tells you that you need to finish writing a report for another colleague who had to go home early. You know that this will take at least an hour. You tell your boss that you would be more than happy to take over for the colleague and to finish the report. You ask when she or he needs to report and, if it is that day, you get it finished before you leave. If the report is not needed until Monday, tell your boss that you still need to finish your own deadlines, but you would be happy to work on the report over the weekend and have it to him or her first thing Monday morning. Before you deliver the report, look critically at your workload and, if this is a task you can comfortably take on, and if this is a colleague who often leaves work for others to finish, offer to take over this report to free up the other person to concentrate on the rest of their workload.

Scenario B

Your car breaks down for the fifth time in four months. You have already spent over two thousand dollars at the repair shop and have been late to work several times because of it. You realize that this is not a workable solution, that you are wasting money, and you need to define and evaluate your other options. Is there reliable public transportation that you can avail yourself of in order to get to work every day? Is there a ride share program in the area? Does someone at your work live near you, and you can ride with them in exchange for gas money? Is your job close enough to bike to work each day? Can you trade your car in on a newer model (a reliable used car), or does your budget allow you to purchase a reasonably priced new car?

Scenario C

Your brother calls you and says that he was fired (again) from his job and asks if he can come crash at your place, just until he gets back on his feet. The last three times he did this, it was always for at least a month, and he never cleaned, never helped with bills or groceries, and left his laundry for you to do. You know that this time will be exactly the same unless you are proactive and lay down some house rules. You tell him that you need to call him back in ten minutes. You take that time to write a list of house rules that address all of the problems and concerns you have had with him in the past. You take a picture of the list and text it to him, then call him to go over the house rules. If he agrees to follow all of them, then he can come to stay. If he does not, then he needs to find another place to stay.

If your responses were similar to these, well done, you are already thinking like the Winner that you are. If your responses were different, how could you change your thinking and your mindset so that the next time you are faced with a similar situation, you react as a Winner and not as a whiner? Notice how in each scenario, the response was to be proactive, have a solution, and not to whine about it?

Until you have your own business, where you are the sole person in charge of every decision, you will be faced with scenarios like these at work, and will have to respond to them. Just as in your dress and your bearing, you need to be the Winner that you are when you transact with other people in both your professional and your personal lives.

Begin to respond to everyone, whether professionally or personally, in the same way: with a positive, problem solving attitude where you take charge of situations and turn them around in order to get the outcome that you want. Do not let others control situations for you, but figure out how to make them want to agree to your ideas and your solutions. This is how Winners handle contention and disputes in their lives: they do not complain about them, but change the situation to suit them.

CHAPTER 10

Failure is Necessary

Winners are going to fail. What separates them from everyone else is that they do not stop with failure, but turn that failure into a path to success.

One of the hardest things in life is failing. Failing at something can eat away at your self confidence, it can make you question the choices that you are making, and it can make you change the path that you have mapped out in a negative direction. Is does not matter if the failure is in your professional life or in your personal one; the results are the same. Doubt. Loss of self-esteem. Losing sight of the Right Mindset. Thinking that you are not a Winner.

However, failure is necessary in order to become a Winner. Read that sentence again: failure is necessary in order to become a Winner. Everyone is going to fail at something at one point in their life. How they react to that failure is what defines them.

When you fail, do you moan and complain about how unfair life is, how the system is stacked against you, how it was not your fault? Or, when you fail, do you use it as an opportunity to learn from your mistake? Do you look at the failure with an objective lens and begin to make a plan for how to avoid the same errors the next time? Failure is rarely the fault of a single individual. Usually, all sides share in some of the responsibility of having failed. You need to identify what you did wrong, or what you failed to do, and make sure that you do not make the same mistake the next time.

James Dyson is one of the most well known entrepreneurs and inventors of our time because of his revolutionary vacuum machine design, but what many people do not know is that he was rejected an astonishing 5,126 times before he had any success in marketing and selling his creation. Now, most people do not have to face such a staggering amount of rejection when they begin to create their own business, but they do have to face some amount of rejection.

Like a true Winner, every time James Dyson was rejected, he used the opportunity to learn from that particular failure. He went back to his workshop, reviewed at how he had failed, looked critically at his design, took the information from his rejection, and used his new knowledge to change his design until he finally had the perfect product.

You must prepare yourself to not be completely successful the very first time you enter the marketplace. How will you handle failure? How will you handle rejection? How would a Winner deal with these situations? When someone rejects your idea or your proposal, here are several comebacks that you need to have ready.

- I am sorry that we could not work together at this time. I hope that you will keep me in mind when you are ready to expand your company and client base, and I will check back in with you next month.

- I am sorry to hear that now is not a good time for you to take on an investment like this. Please keep me in mind when your company is ready to expand into the digital market, and I will check back in with you next month.

- I am sorry that now is not the right time for you and your company. I would love to work with you in the future, so please let me know when you are ready for a change, and I will check back in with you next month.

Begin practicing meeting a rejection in this way so that, by the time you are ready to pitch your first product or service, your reply will be automatic. You can do this in your day to day interactions at work, with friends, or in other social situations.

For example:

- I am sorry that we could not connect while you were in town because of our differing schedules. I hope that you will keep me in mind when you are back in the city, and we can meet up for lunch or drinks, and I will check back in with you next month.

- I am sorry to hear that now is not a good time for you to take on a responsibility and time commitment like this. Please keep me in mind for when your schedule opens up, and you have more time to volunteer because we would love to have you join our team, and I will check back in with you next month.

- I am sorry that now is not the right time for you and your team to join our after work league. I would love to work with you in the future, so please let me know when you are ready for a change and I will check back in with you next month.

Do not see rejection as a closing door, but as an opportunity for another, or a different possibility. Always answer somebody's rejection by turning it around so that you are the one in charge, you are the one who is offering them an opportunity, and you are the one who will be getting back in touch with them. Notice that, no matter what the circumstance is, each response sees you as the one in control? Every response begins with "I" because you are taking charge of the conversation, and every response ends with you being the one to get back in touch with the other party, again an example of you being in charge.

You are the one who is going to touch base with them in the next month (or whatever time frame is appropriate for the circumstances). In this manner, you are in control, and you retain that control, even if they reject your first offer or idea.

Remember that Winners take rejection and turn it into an opportunity.

CHAPTER 11

Never Stop

Winners are always working on themselves and their goals because they know that they can always get better, always improve, and always continue to work harder.

Would you say that you are a perfect person? If you answered that honestly, you would have answered "no." No one is perfect. Everyone has areas of themselves and their lives that they could improve upon, and Winners are no different.

Look at some of the top athletes in the world, people who embody the term "Winner" and who have made a success of themselves and their lives. When I think about this group of individuals, one person that immediately comes to mind is Emmaniel Dapidran Pacquiao, or Manny Pacquiao. If you have never heard of Manny Pacquiao, he is considered to be one of the best boxers ever to fight in the sport. Coming from the Phillipines, Manny Pacquiao is the epitome of the word "Winner," not just as a boxer, or as a politician, or as an actor, but as an individual.

Some people might think after having won every award that he has won, and earned the success that he now enjoys, Manny Pacquiao would stop working so hard and just enjoy his success. That could not be further from the truth. Every day he wakes up and continues to work on himself, both physically, mentally, and spiritually, work on his businesses, and work on his family. Manny Pacquiao understands that in order to be a Winner, you can never stop working, you can never stop striving, and you can never stop aiming for your goals. When you achieve one goal, you form another goal and work towards it.

There will always be people who look to you for guidance and direction, whether you realize it or not, and that is the hallmark of a true Winner: when you have others who see your success and want to emulate you because of how successful you are.

When you have achieved one of your goals for being a Winner (those are the three Winner affirmations that you wrote out and have been repeating to yourself every day), replace that goal with another one. Go back to the same list that you created of things about yourself that you want to change, and make another positive WINNER affirmation and replace each copy of the goal you already attained with the new one (next to your bed, in your dressing area, on the back of your front door, and in your briefcase, laptop bag, or day planner).

You should always have three goals about yourself that you are working on and, as you achieve one goal, replace it with another. Do not, however, throw away the papers with the goals that you have achieved written on them. Place these goals next to your Dream Life goal (on your stair climbing machine, on the kitchen table where you sit to have coffee and read every morning, or on the mirror of the bathroom – wherever you posted it).

In this way, you will be able to visually see how working on yourself and your personal WINNER goals, and achieving those goals, is bringing you closer and closer to your reaching your Dream Life and being the person that you have always wanted to be: successful, focused, and a Winner.

By looking back at these goals every day as you reread your Dream Life goal and visualize it, you will also be reminded of the hard work that you have already done and of the goals that you have already achieved. If there is no concrete thing to look at, like a trophy or a plaque, sometimes it is easy to forget all of the hard work, sweat equity, and dedication you have already given towards achieving your goals and your Dream Life.

You will always be working on yourself and your goals because being a Winner does not stop with achieving your first goal, or even your second. Being a Winner is not a goal in and of itself, but who you are inside, every moment and every minute of every day. Just like you would not stop working at your own business after you made your first profit, why would you stop working on yourself after you become successful?

The short answer is that you would not.

You will always find yourself working on yourself, working to be better, working to do better, and working to create better, because that is what a Winner does. Winners do not give up. We are constantly looking to improve ourselves and our lives because we know that this is an ongoing effort, not a single sprint toward success, but an endurance marathon that we will constantly be participating in.

Winners never stop learning: learning from their mistakes, learning from their mentors, and learning from the mistakes of others. Who is your mentor? Who is someone that you look up to and think to yourself, "I want to be like that person"? What is it about that person that makes them someone you admire? Take a few minutes and think about what it is about that person that you admire and put those thoughts into concrete words.

Take this book and get something to write with (pencil, pen, et cetera) and either sticky notes, paper, and tape, or use your computer and printer. At the top of the page, write the name of the person you admire, or the name of the person who is your mentor. If you have more than one, give each person their own page.

For example:

Charles Clinton Spaulding	Cindy Mi

Next, under the person's name, write down their character traits, quotes they have said, or other items that showcase why you think so highly of them.

For example:

Charles Clinton Spaulding	Cindy Mi

· started out as a dishwasher, but kept working hard and became the president of North Carolina Mutual Insurance Company	· taught herself English when she was a teenager
· had a reputation of being honest, having integrity, and was a natural business man	· dropped out of high school and founded her first company
· hired teachers and promoted small businesses in his community; was always giving back	· earned her MBA and started her second company, which is now a world wide educational teaching and tutoring company
· "I believe in the promise of America, which can only be realized through sweat, thrift, and enterprise; do not expect something for nothing."	· "Make the decision and do not come back in tears. I need to be responsible for what I am getting into in life."

You are going to make mistakes, and you will even fail in some areas of starting your own business. I am not saying this to make you feel defeated or to suggest that you cannot do this. You can do this. You will do this.

I am telling you this so that you will be prepared for when it happens. One of the worst things that you could do when starting your own business is to be told that it is easy, that you will be a phenomenal success, and that you will not fail. If someone tells you this, they are lying to you.

Yes, you will fail. That is completely natural when it comes to starting your own business. There is not a successful business person out there, man or woman, who did not fail at the beginning. (Many of them still have failures, because taking risks and chances are what it takes to continue to grow and continue to be a success.)

I would not be helping you at all if I told you that you would not fail. You will fail. How I am helping you is to help you format a plan for when you fail so that you can turn that failure into a success. Winners learn from every time they do not get something right. Every failure is an opportunity to grow, to learn, and to succeed in your next attempt.

When you make a mistake or make a choice that leads to the wrong outcome, I want you to look back at the sheet you made for your mentor and I want you to ask yourself, "What would he (or she) do to fix this?" "How would she (or he) solve this problem and get back on track towards growing this business?" "What would he (or she) say to me if they were here right now?"

Every time you make a mistake, or go in the wrong direction, stop, analyze the mistake, and figure out how to not make the same mistake again. Ask yourself the following questions:

· What led me to this point?

· Were there warning signs that I ignored? If so, why did I ignore the signs? How can I keep from making the same mistake in the future?

· Did I know that this was the wrong path from the beginning? If so, why did I still choose to do this? Was it pride? Did I trust the wrong person? Did I not have complete control over the business?

· How will I avoid this mistake in the future? What procedures or routines do I need to put in place in order to prevent this from happening again?

· Is there someone I need to apologize to because they are affected by this?

That last question is one of the hardest questions for a lot of people and this is something that I personally have never understood. Why is it so difficult to apologize to another individual? An apology does not make you a weak person. Quite the contrary: an apology often makes you the stronger person, because you not only saw that you did something wrong, you did not try to cover it up or refuse to acknowledge it. Instead, you identified your error, went to the person whom you had wronged, and apologized for the mistake.

In business, most people are taken aback whenever someone apologizes, because they do not expect it. Our business world has gotten to the point where most people refuse to apologize when an apology will often gain you the respect and admiration of others.

Think of the last time someone looked you in the eye and apologized for something that they had done or something that they had forgotten to do. Think of how much respect you had for them at that moment, and probably still do.

Being a Winner does not mean that you are always right, but, rather, that you always try to do the right thing.

Part 2: Repeatable Path

Ideas are only the beginning. Winners take their ideas and turn them into opportunities and businesses.

I am going to be honest with you, and it is something that you need to hear. If it were really easy to make money, everyone would be rich. People who are millionaires and billionaires, ones who made their fortune and did not inherit it or fall into it by winning the lottery, all achieved their wealth by turning an idea into an opportunity.

Ideas are plentiful, like pebbles on a lake shore or sand on the beach. Everyone has ideas, for improving the efficiency of a household item, for ending global warming, for reducing the time you waste sitting in traffic being unproductive. Some people even fill notebooks full of ideas or bore their friends and loved ones with endless conversations on the topic.

Winners take their ideas and turn them into opportunities. Joy Mangano is a woman who has had many, many ideas for improving household items, for inventing new items, and for modifying existing inventions to be more efficient, stronger, last longer, or to work better. She is best known for making a mop that wrings itself, an invention she created after growing frustrated with hand wringing the standard wet, dirty, heavy mop everyone was using at the time.

Joy Mangano is a Winner who had an idea and turned that idea into an opportunity. Once she had the idea for a new invention, she did not leave it there, proceeding to bore everyone she knew for the next ten years with a "could have, should have, would have" story of the idea she had, but never did anything with. Instead, she saved up money, created her product, went to trade shows to sell it, and made her Dream Life happen.

Joy Mangano is good at thinking of inventions and ways to improve people's daily lives. What are you good at? This is where your idea will come from.

Take a moment, and think about what you are good at doing, what talents you have, what skills you can offer others. Take this book and get something to write with (pencil, pen, et cetera) and either sticky notes, paper, and tape, or use your computer and printer.

Do you have everything ready? No, then stop reading and go get the items you need. Remember, Winners are always ready and willing to do the work that needs to be done. Do not procrastinate by saying "I will just finish reading this, and then I will go do it." No, you will not. Saying that is the start to making excuses. Winners act. They do not make excuses, so go get your things.

Now that you are ready, make a list of all the things that you do well, no matter how silly or trivial you think they may be. Think of all areas of your life (home, work, friends, shopping, exercising, traveling, reading, hobbies, family, et cetera) and what it is that you do well in each of them. Write each item down.

For example:

- painting life-size portraits of pets
- organizing kitchen spices
- playing the guitar
- finding efficient routes for driving
- altering clothes to fit better
- turning leftovers into tasty new lunches
- summarizing boring reports into short, understandable paragraphs
- setting up the technology for a video conference, including remotely
- making guests feel welcome and at home
- baking tasty biscuits
- creating a comfortable, productive, and efficient home office using minimal space
- turning a piece of furniture into a multiple purpose item
- reading books to children using a variety of voices

- choosing clothes for others that fit their personality and style perfectly

- teaching people how to cook Ecuadorian food

Remember, you are not writing a list of items from a single category or with a common theme. Nor are you trying to think about making money, time investments, or marketing. This is not a business plan. You are just writing down everything that you do well as a brainstorming activity.

Read the list to yourself and add more ideas to it as you think of them. Take a tour around your home, look at your daily and weekly schedule, and take a virtual walk through your entire life, thinking about what you do on a daily or weekly basis, and add more items to your list. You should have a few dozen traits and activities by the time you are finished.

CHAPTER 12

Turning an Idea Into a Service

Turn your idea into a service that you can offer to others, one that they will pay for time and time again.

Now, look at your list with an objective lens. What are items on your list that can be turned into services for others? What did you write down that can become a commodity, to be sold to other individuals?

Highlight these items on your list. Next, write each item as a heading on its own piece of paper. Here is where you will begin actually planning, turning your ideas into opportunities.

For example, here are four sheets with the titles:

baking tasty biscuits	teaching people how to cook Ecuadorian food
painting life size portraits of pets	making guests feel welcome and at home

Now, here are the sheets with notes on how to turn these ideas into opportunities:

baking tasty, cravable biscuits	playing the guitar
· Find out if there are any biscuit shops in the neighborhood. · What does it take to get a food permit in the county? In the city? · Is there an existing food truck hose food these would compliment? An existing restaurant?	· Do I do this well enough to make a career out of it? If so, is that what I want to do? · Does anyone in the neighborhood (or city) offer lessons? Do any of the local day cares offer art lessons for their children? · Are there coffee shops that could use entertainment?
painting life size portraits of pets	making guests feel welcome and at home
· Find out if there is a local artist already offering this type of painting.	· Find out if there is anyone in the area

- What art galleries in the area wold be best to carry these paintings?

- Is there a boutique pet store that would have the right clientèle for this? Would they be interested in a partnership? Does their store have room for a display (painting and business cards)?

- Would they be willing to partner with me if I offered a monthly class to their customers?

- Are there more than one of these kinds of boutiques in the area?

offering this kind of hospitality service.

- Who would be my reference clientèle? Traveling business executives? Wealthy people having guests stay with them?

- Is there a "live work play" neighborhood (or more than one) that would have my target audience?

- Could I offer a menu of services?

Look at the sheets you made with headings and begin to make notes. These notes may be further ideas, questions, or anything that occurs to you. The more you write, the more you will see the opportunities and how that particular idea can become the path to your Dream Life.

Please remember that you are making these notes as the next step in this process. Do not pick a single idea and focus solely on it but, instead, have several ideas that you are "fleshing out." This will ensure that you do not lock yourself into a set path, and it will allow you to be flexible.

Also, most entrepreneurs and people of wealth do not have a single cash flow system or a single job that they do. You may find that when you turn one idea into an opportunity, you are only using three or four hours of a single day, leaving you with more time to pursue other avenues of opportunity and money.

As you write each item down, consider these questions:

- Do I need a business license to become incorporated or an LLC (limited liability company)?

- Does what I am offering or doing need a permit or license?

- Does this service already exist in the neighborhood or city? If so, are there enough people willing to pay for it to support another business?

- Who is my target audience or clientèle? How do I connect with them?

- Logistically, what do I need to do to create this product or service? Where is the best place to get these for the best price?

- Is there a small business group in my area that can help me get started? Are there people that I can network with? Do I already know someone with a complementary business, or a similar one, that I can talk to?

- How will I promote this service or business? Is there a local network for business advertisements? Do I need business cards or brochures?

- What will I charge for this service?

Look back on the list that you made. What are items on your list that can be turned into products that others would want to buy? What did you write down that can become a commodity, to be sold to other individuals?

Highlight these items on your list. Next, write each item as a heading on its own piece of paper. Here you will once again turn your ideas into opportunities, this time for products instead of services.

For example, here are four sheets with the titles:

create a tablet screen that can easily be customizable to any tablet and withstands impacts of up to thirty pounds	build a playground set that can be used by sight impaired children
make an all facial natural moisturizer for men that works with facial hair	create a platform that creates playlists based on one-word inputs from the user

Just as before, add notes on how to turn these ideas into opportunities by looking critically at each one. For example:

create a tablet screen that can easily be customizable to any tablet and withstands impacts of up to thirty pounds	**build a playground set that can be used by sight impaired children**
· Have I tested this out on enough tablets to be confident that it works? Have I tried this with both children and adults? · What do I need to do to file a patent?	· Is this different than any product currently on the market? · Have I tested this out to be sure of safety and usefulness? · What do I need to do to file a patent?

· Who would be my target audience? Individuals? Companies? Schools?	· What are the safety regulations that I need to follow? · Who is my target audience? Schools for the blind? Public parks? Community playgrounds? · Can this be used by seeing children as well?
make an all natural facial moisturizer for men that works with facial hair · Have I tested this on all skin and hair types? · Is there a similar item on the market? If so, how is mine different or better? · What do I need to do to file a patent? · Do I need a trademark? · Do I need copyright?	**design an app that creates playlists based on one-word inputs from the user** · What do I need to do to file a patent? · Will this work on all devices and with all music services? · How will I continue to improve this system? · Will user input be multiple-choice, picture based, or something else? · Have I extensively tested this out with people of all

	different likes, types, and styles? Did I evaluate their feedback?

As you write each item down, consider these questions:

· Do I need a business license to become incorporated or an LLC (limited liability company)?

· Do I need a patent or a license from any government agency?

· Does this product already exist in the open market? If so, how is my design better or different?

· Who is my target audience or clientèle? How do I connect with them?

· Logistically, what do I need to do to create this product? Where is the best place to get these made for the best price?

· Is there a small business group in my area that can help me get started? Are there people that I can network with? Do I already know someone with a complementary business, or a similar one, that I can talk to?

· How will I promote this product? Is there a local network for business advertisements? Do I need business cards or brochures?

- What will I charge for this product?

- How will I distribute this product? What packaging and materials do I need? Where can I find the best price for them?

- Will I sell this directly, like at trade shows, or wholesale to companies and businesses? Should I sell online, like through market places such as eBay, Shopify, Rakuten, Etsy, Bonanza, Newegg, or Amazon?

- Is there a Better Business Bureau or Small Business Commission or Chamber of Commerce that can help you answer these questions? Can they help you network your business?

CHAPTER 13

Where to Start

Winners are serious about winning. Life is not a game, and living your Dream Life is not a luxury, but a necessity. You need to be able to depend upon yourself for your own retirement.

Is this just a fun read for you, did you download this book on a lark, or are you truly serious about changing your life, taking control of your destiny, and making your Dream Life a reality? If you are serious, and you are already doing the work, one important area you need to address is your home office space.

You may be blessed to have an entire room where you have put a desk, a computer, a printer, and all of the other accouterments that you need, or you may live in a very small place where space is at a premium, and you are making do by working on a TV tray. The size of your home office does not matter as much as its location and its organization.

You need an office space that is free from distractions, quiet so that you can be focused and organized so that you know where everything is and can put your finger on any needed item in an instant.

Let us begin with the first item: free from distractions. Your home office should be located in an area where others are not going to be walking or passing through and interrupting you, where there is no television on providing a distraction, and where outside distractions, such as from glass doors or windows, are not going to be an issue. Your home office should be in the quietest room, or area, of your home. If this is your bedroom, because that is the only room with a door and no television, then go for it. Choose a room that others will not need access to while you are working and that is free from distractions.

Next, make sure that your home office space is free of extraneous noise. If there is a television that you can hear, and you get distracted by such things, make sure that it is turned off. Before you begin working, make sure that there are no alarms that are going to go off and disturb you, make sure that you are not situated next to a window with a tree filled with noisy birds, and make sure that you are not trying to multi task by cooking dinner and working at the same time.

The last item you need to look at is organization. If you have a dedicated home office space, you will need a board (such as a bulletin board, cork board or white board) to keep track of your ideas, timelines, and the bigger picture. If you do not have a dedicated room for this and are using your bedroom or living room (and do not have a wall that you can leave the board up on all of the time) you will need a board that can be taken out, used, then put away behind a headboard or under a couch. You need to have an organizer, date book, or calendar that you use to keep track of meetings, dead lines, shipments when to connect back with people, and other essential business items. You will also need an actual workspace for your work, whether it is a place to paint, a commissary to bake in, or a workshop in which to build your product.

At the beginning of your business, you may be able to make do with space you have in your existing home. If, however, as time goes on and your business begins to grow, and you have more capital to invest back into the business, you may need to look for other options, such as renting garage or storage space, finding a work share space, or moving into a bigger place that includes plenty of room for your personal life as well as your business.

CHAPTER 14

The Logistics

Remember that time is your first asset; money is your second asset. You have to spend money in order to make money. How will you finance your business?

If you are living from paycheck to paycheck, with less than a month's worth of salary in your bank account, you are not ready to start your own business. Starting a business means that you need capital or funds with which to pay for licenses, permits, products, advertising, business cards, stock, travel expenses . . . the list goes on and on. Without money in the bank with which to pay for all of these things, and more, you will not be able to start your business and really make a go of it. Before you begin, you need to make sure that you have enough money for your business to work.

One way to finance your business is to take out a loan, either from a bank, a financial institution, or an investor. If you decide to take out a loan, make sure that you know the terms of the loan upfront, from the interest rate that you will be charged to the payment schedule and the terms of repayment. The one major benefit of taking out a loan is that you have all your capital before you begin, and you can proceed with all of your financings. The one major drawback to taking out a loan is that your business will have to turn a profit from the very first month, something that is not very common, and you will have the added expense of the loan payment each month.

Another way is to get a small business grant from either the government, an organization or foundation, or from your local Office of Economic Development. Grants can be like loans, in that they have to be paid back, or they can be like a scholarship, where you just have to use the money as agreed upon. Another type of grant is the social networking kind, from crowd funding or sourcing platforms. (If you are not familiar with crowd funding and sourcing structures, there is everything available from raising money to designers helping you create graphics or products.)

A third way to finance your business is to have all of the capital on hand by saving for it. This is a slower method to get started on owning your own business, but you have a lot less initial risk since you are not borrowing the money and, thus, having to pay it back to a bank, investor, or another financial institution.

No matter the way you choose, before you begin your business, you need to make sure that your finances are in order. Take this book and get something to write with (pencil, pen, et cetera) and either sticky notes, paper, and tape, or use your computer and printer. Grab your bank account statement, your checkbook, your monthly bills, and any other paperwork that concerns your budget. (If you already have a written budget out, start there. If you do not, you will be making one.)

Create a three column table like this:

Monthly Income	Monthly Expense	Monthly Savings

Under each column, include all of your income sources, your expenses, and how much money you are actually saving. (The "Savings" are monies that you do not touch, but that keep accruing in your bank account. These are not amounts that carry over to the next month, then are spent.)

Under your Expenses column, make sure that you include how much you actually spend in each of the following areas: entertainment, eating out, groceries, toiletries, clothing, household items, personal care, child care, debt, transportation, pet care, medical and medication, miscellaneous expenses

For example:

Monthly Income	Monthly Expense	Monthly Savings
Paycheck from work +$3,497.48	Rent -$1,100.00	Savings -$50.00
	Pet Care -$45.00	
	Phone Bill -$39.00	
	Electric Bill -$78.00	
	Water and Sewer Bill -$50.00	
	Personal Care -$75.00	
	Groceries -$437.46	
	Morning to go coffee	

	-$65.60	
	Medicine -$7.00	
	Toiletries -$17.48	
	Eating Out -$125.46	
	Car Insurance -$116.28	
	Gasoline and Oil Change -$80.00	
	Car Payment -$540.00	
	Clothing -$42.76	
	Credit Card Payment -$90.00	
	Credit Card Payment -$120.00	

	Household Items -$38.35	
	Internet -$20.00	
	Health Insurance -$340.00	

According to this example, you are spending $3,477.39 each month and only earning $3,497.48, leaving you with $20.09 for any expenses that are not accounted for on the above table, for any unexpected expenditures, or for any emergencies.

You cannot start a business with $20.09. (Even if you look at saving this amount every month for a year, you are still nowhere near the capital you need to begin your own business.) Now, if your actual budget is a lot healthier than this one, you are well on your way to being able to afford your own business.

If, however, you are like the majority of people, your budget looks similar to this one. You have to go through a determine what expenses can be pared down, which ones can be eliminated, and which ones can be changed.

The goal of a budget is not so that you are living within your means, but so that you are living below your means. When you live below your means, you are saving money for the future: for your retirement, for starting your own business, for making your Dream Life a reality.

Start with your largest expenses: rent, car payment, and health insurance. You need health insurance, yes, but is there a less expensive option that you could go with? One that would afford you the same, or similar coverage, but for a smaller payment every month?

You need reliable transportation every day. What makes the most sense with your needs and your budget? Is their a local transportation network (buses, rail, or subway) that you could take advantage of that would be cheaper? Is there a ride share program that you could join? Would buying a cheaper, used car make more sense? Are there people in your area who would be willing to car pool in exchange for gas money to help you defray the cost of owning a car?

For most people, the biggest budgetary item is rent or a mortgage. If you are purchasing a home, you need to ask yourself how you could help reduce the cost of the mortgage payment every month. Is your home big enough that you could take on a roommate? Could you refinance for a smaller monthly payment?

If you are renting, is there a less expensive area of town to live in? If you have a two bedroom apartment, could you move into a one bedroom and reduce your rent by a few hundred dollars? Or could you add a roommate who would help pay your rent amount? Are their rentals available in your area that cost the same as what you are currently paying, but that include all utilities?

Some of these questions will not be easy, and you may not want to ask them, but when you are looking at starting your own business and becoming financially independent, these are the questions that need to be asked. The reason why most people are in debt is that they are not willing to live within their means, let alone below their means.

CHAPTER 15

Budgeting

Winners are never frivolous or thoughtless when it comes to money. They do everything with intent and with keeping an eye towards their future.

The next section of your budget to look at are the frivolous expenses. These are the expenses that seem small at the time but can add up quite quickly. For example, look at the morning to go coffee and the eating out expenses. Combined, if you eliminated those two from your budget, you would save $191.06 every month. Add that to your $20.09, and you suddenly go from having an extra $241.08 a year (by saving $20.09 each month) to having $2,533.80 a year. That is a tremendous difference!

You cannot start your own business with $241.08, but you could with $2,533.80. All it took you was making coffee at home instead of stopping at the coffee shop and not eating out. Instead, begin a bi-monthly house dinner party with your circle of friends, with each friend hosting it once every other month. When it is your turn, you can easily use your normal groceries to host a dinner party for four or six, it will not cost you anything extra in your budget, and you are saving over $2,000.00 a year.

When you are making $3,497.48 a month, or whatever amount you are actually bringing home, your savings on hand should be at least six times that amount, or $20,984.88. This may seem like a luxury, but it is not. You should have six months of earnings in your savings account, or in your bank account, to guard against the unexpected.

As recent history has shown us, you can never predict what will happen in the world, and you need to be prepared for whatever may come your way with at least six months' worth of income on hand. This will ensure that, when you begin your own business, you will be able to weather and withstand any economic emergencies that occur, whether they stem from the global economy or are more locally pinpointed.

How do you amass a savings equivalent to six months' of your take home pay? It is actually quite easy. The first step is living below your means, not at or above them. All of the extra money in your budget should immediately go towards that savings. What do you spend money on each month that is not necessary? An entertainment service? A subscription service? A gym membership? Even a modest monthly payment of $20 adds up to $240 every year.

When was the last time you bargain shopped or made a price comparison? Is there an online service that is cheaper than what you are currently paying for your grooming supplies? Could you go to the salon every five weeks instead of every four? Is there a less expensive car insurance option? Look back at your budget and ask yourself where you are needlessly spending money and where you can save money every month.

CHAPTER 16

Avoid Debt

Winners do not pay others money needlessly or give it away thoughtlessly because they understand the value of money and the hard work and effort it took to earn it.

Another topic to bring up, that not many people consider is the use of credit cards and bank cards. We are moving towards a global economy that is more and more electronically based and relies less on actual paper money and coins. This is not always to the benefit of the consumer. It is far too easy to swipe a plastic card at the grocery store or a restaurant and, when the monthly statement arrives in the mail, to merely pay the minimum.

This is not what Winners do. Winners are not in debt, they do not buy things that they cannot afford, and they pay for everything up front. This is a very difficult concept for some people because it seems counter intuitive, but this is how the truly wealthy operate. Why would you ever pay interest to a company just to use their credit card each month? If you do use a credit card, you should be paying it off every month. (And, if you do use a credit card, you should be getting something out of it, like frequent flier miles or rewards points that you can use in exchange for commodities that you want.)

If you do not use a credit card, make sure that you are not substituting your bank card for one. This is another trap that people fall into when it concerns their money. The best way to save money is to give yourself an "allowance" every month and pay cash for everything that you purchase.

When I began to plan my own business, and I needed to finance it, this is exactly what I did. As competitive as I am, I even made a game out of it, trying to see how much money I had left at the end of the month from my "allowance" and putting that money straight into savings. When you do this, you will be amazed at what you end up spending because you are no longer spending money in an abstract way by using credit cards, but in a concrete way by counting out bills and handing the money over in exchange for goods and services.

You will also be pleasantly surprised to find that you no longer need to spend as much as you have been. When I went to a cash only system, I went from spending over a hundred dollars a week on groceries to averaging around sixty dollars each week. The $40 savings added up to $2,080 in the first year. That is nearly ten percent of the six months' savings we just discussed.

Winners use banks, not money lending services or cash checking services, to conduct their business transactions because you should never pay for your own money. Now, everything that I have mentioned in this section has revolved around a bank account, and that is a very deliberate action. Nearly twenty five percent (25%!) of people do not have a bank account. This is one of the biggest mistakes that you can make with your money. Why? Quite easily; you are paying other people to do things that you should be getting for free.

Opening up a bank account should be like shopping for shoes or a car. You do not want to only go to one store or dealership, but you want to shop around. Try different options out. Talk to the salespeople. My simple rules for opening up a checking account are:

1. **NEVER pay a monthly fee.** Why would you give someone else your money *and* pay them to take it? There are banks and credit unions that will even pay you to open up an account. Do not accept any monthly fees, ever, and, if your bank tries to start a "new policy," where they will charge you

a monthly fee, then you know that it is time to move to a new bank.

2. **Always use your checking account like a savings account.** Yes, it is true that you will not earn any interest this way, but you should always have at least six months' salary on hand in your checking account.

3. **If you have a savings account, make sure that you are earning the most you can on it.** The bank is using your money to make themselves money, so if you have a savings account, make sure you are getting the best rate and check that rate every quarter to see if you can get a better one.

People who do not have a checking account are cashing their checks in other ways, normally with a check cashing service, and that means that they are paying other people to do what a bank will do for free. Also, without a banking account, most people have to purchase money orders to pay their bills, and, again, this is paying someone else to do something that a bank will do for free.

CHAPTER 17:

Be Self-Reliant

Winners rely on themselves to achieve success, not on others, because they know that they are the ones who will reap the rewards.

I am sure that you have heard the phrase "there is no such thing as a free lunch" and, to me, this catchphrase has always meant that no one is going to give you anything. Owning your own business and being in charge of your goals and your Dream Life is the same. No one is going to make your dreams come true except for you. You are the only one you can depend on to make this happen. You are the only one who will work towards achieving your goals and towards attaining the Dream Life that you have envisioned. No one will do this for you.

Why? The answer is easy. No one will be invested in making your Dream Life a reality because it is **your** Dream Life, no one else's. Everyone has their own goals and their own Dream Life, but the majority of people never achieve their goals and never live their Dream Life. Why? People expect things to be giving to them in life.

People have a sense of entitlement that they are *owed* everything that comes their way. This is not how Winners think. Winners know that the only thing you will ever get for free in life is a tax bill at the end of the year. If you want to achieve your goals and make your Dream Life a reality, then you will have to be the one who makes it happen.

Winners are successful because they understand this, and they know that no one is going to do it for them. The only person you can rely on is yourself. You know what is at stake, you know how much hard work it is going to take, and you know what the rewards will be when you achieve every goal you have put into place and when you fully realize your Dream Life.

In order to make sure that you are the one in charge of your own destiny, your own goals, and your own Dream Life, you need to be as independent as possible in your life and in your business.

When you depend upon others for any part of your business, you are giving up some of that independence and allowing others to be in charge. This may be alright if it is someone that you can trust with your very life, for that is what you are doing. Your business is your life and, when you put part of its control in the hands of another, you are putting part of your life in their care and keeping.

If, however, you do not trust them that deeply, that is not a bad thing. You should be wary of others and their motives. At any time, someone else could come along and offer your supplier more money for the same product that was promised to you and, before you know it, your shipment of supplies has been delayed by three months or, even worse, canceled all together.

When you are creating plans for your business, always have a backup plan, or two, for every aspect of your company. This will ensure that, when people let you down, and they will, your business will not be harmed because you have had the presence of mind to implement fail safes and back up contingency plans.

When you find a supplier for materials that you need, make sure that you have a second and third supplier on hand for when the first one can no longer deliver what your business needs. When you assign a delivery system for your product and have everything ready to go, make sure that you have an alternate waiting for when the first one does not work out, because they are over extended because their workers went on strike, or for whatever reason they have for not being able to fulfill your needs.

By having alternatives and contingencies in place, you will ensure that you retain your independence, and your business is truly your own; that no outside force or company can consciously or unintentionally harm your hard work and planning.

The same plans need to be implemented when it comes to employees. If your business grows beyond what you can do yourself, and you need to hire employees to work for you, remember to have contingency plans in place. What will you do if an employee calls in sick, does not show up, or just arbitrarily quits? Do you have another ready to hire immediately? Have you been in contact with staffing agencies and temporary placement services, so that they can quickly fill your needs?

Just as I have cautioned you to make sure that you have thought about everything that could go wrong in other areas and to plan for it, you need to look critically at the areas of your business that rely on others and make sure that you have a plan for when those others will let you down or fail to fulfill their contracts or promises. In this way, you will truly be independent, and your business will really be your own.

CHAPTER 18

Responding to a Change of Plans

Winners are like coaches: they always have a backup plan for when the first plan fails to be a success because the first plan almost always fails.

Just as we have talked about how Winners and wealthy people are not always successful when they first begin to create their own business, they also have more than one revenue stream, more than one way to make money. Winners are very similar to any coach of any sports team or event. They make several plans, or plays, and have their players practice them because they know that the first one or two will not always be successful.

Take this book with you and gather together your notes from when you brainstormed turning your ideas into opportunities. Are there opportunities that compliment each other or that can be implemented using similar methods, strategies, or even resources?

For example, look at the following list:

- painting life size portraits of pets

- organizing kitchen spices

- playing the guitar

- finding efficient routes for driving

- altering clothes to fit better

- turning leftovers into tasty new lunches

- summarizing boring reports into short, understandable paragraphs

- setting up the technology for a video conference, including remotely

- making guests feel welcome and at home

- baking tasty, cravable biscuits

- creating a comfortable, productive, and efficient home office using minimal space

- turning a piece of furniture into a multiple purpose item

- reading books to children using a variety of voices

- choosing clothes for others that fit their personality and style perfectly

- teaching people how to cook Ecuadorian food

At first glance, the items on the list may not have anything in common, but take a closer look.

- painting life size portraits of pets

- organizing kitchen spices

- playing the guitar

- **finding efficient routes for driving**

- altering clothes to fit better

- turning leftovers into tasty new lunches

- summarizing boring reports into short, understandable paragraphs

- **setting up the technology for a video conference, including remotely**

- making guests feel welcome and at home

- baking tasty, cravable biscuits

- creating a comfortable, productive, and efficient home office using minimal space

- turning a piece of furniture into a multiple purpose item

- **reading books to children using a variety of voices**

- choosing clothes for others that fit their personality and style perfectly

- **teaching people how to cook Ecuadorian food**

The ideas that I have highlighted in **bold** are all ones that can be turned into business opportunities using technology and, what is more important, using the same technology platform, reducing your investment and infrastructure. When you can build more than one revenue stream, or business opportunity, using the same methods or resources, not only are you conserving your money and your investments, but you are utilizing all of the possibilities available to you in a smart fashion, just as a Winner does. Take advantage of any advantage you can get when it comes to business and business deals.

- painting life size portraits of pets

- **organizing kitchen spices**

- playing the guitar

- **finding efficient routes for driving**

- altering clothes to fit better

- turning leftovers into tasty new lunches

- **summarizing boring reports into short, understandable paragraphs**

- **setting up the technology for a video conference, including remotely**

- **making guests feel welcome and at home**

- baking tasty, cravable biscuits

- **creating a comfortable, productive, and efficient home office using minimal space**

- **turning a piece of furniture into a multiple purpose item**

- reading books to children using a variety of voices

- **choosing clothes for others that fit their personality and style perfectly**

- teaching people how to cook Ecuadorian food

Look at the exact same list again, only this time I have placed in **bold** items that are all about organization. If your business is about offering a service, it would be quite easy to offer your organizational services to a variety of clients, extending your market and your opportunities.

Now go get something to write with (pencil, pen, et cetera), highlighters, and either sticky notes, paper and tape, or use your computer and printer. Look at your lists of ideas and opportunities. Identify the ones that share a common theme, or core, and can be turned into your own businesses using some of the same principles, resources, or steps.

Why is this step so critical to the success of starting your own business? Quite simply, because plans never seem to work out the way you plan for them to work. You need to have a backup plan, or contingency plan for starting your own business, just like you will have contingencies for all aspects of your business. Beginning, or starting it, should be no different. You need to have a contingency plan, or a backup plan, in place before you begin your business.

If you plan for failure, you will not actually fail, because you will already be expecting something to go wrong and when it does, you will have another plan already organized and arranged that you can immediately implement. You cannot control the stock market, the economy, the government, or what others will do, but you can control what you will do, what you have planned, and how you will respond to any difficulties and downturns that you will face.

CHAPTER 19:

Research

How do you know which products or services that you have an idea for will be the right ones to turn into an opportunity and make as the center for your own business?

When you have an idea and take that idea and turn it into an opportunity, you want that opportunity to have the best chance that it can. No one wants to create a business only to see it fail. In order to give your business every chance of success, you need to make sure that you have a product or a service that people actually want, that people actually need and that they will pay money for not once, but again and again. How will you determine this? Through the process of Market Research.

Market Research is making sure that your idea and opportunity have validity, that you have an audience and a customer base for it, and that you and your business will both be a success.

Market Research is not your friends or your family telling you that you have a really great barbecue brisket and you should open up your own barbecue restaurant. Market Research does not rely on the opinions of people you know, because they are not objective consumers who will give you honest feedback and answers to your questions. Never use people you know for Market Research because their opinions will skew your results, and you want an objective, non emotional information from your real customer base.

Have you ever gone to a grocery store, and someone had a table set up at the end of one of the aisles, and they were handing out free samples? Companies do not give away free food for the fun of it; they do it because they are conducting market research. The food company has sent out representatives to conduct Market Research on their target audience in order to see if their newest product idea will be successful and if there is a market for it.

You do not want to waste all of your capital and the money you have saved to start your own business by failing to conduct Market Research, starting your business, only to realize that there is no market for the product or the service that you are offering.

How will you conduct your own Market Research? First, you need to identify your target consumer. Who is it that will be purchasing your product or your service, really?

Take this book and get something to write with (pencil, pen, et cetera) and either sticky notes, paper, and tape, or use your computer and printer. Also, gather the lists that you wrote out for starting your own business.

Look back on the lists that you made of your ideas and the opportunities that you could turn those ideas into. For the main ideas that you have identified as the best possibilities, who is your target audience? Who has the money and the need for that product or that service? Take the ideas, or opportunities, that you have identified as the ones with which to create your own business and put each one on its own sheet of paper.

For example, here are four sheets with the business opportunities:

altering clothes to fit better	reading books to children using a variety of voices
teaching people how to cook Ecuadorian food	painting life size portraits of pets

Now, here are the sheets with notes on who may be the target audience:

altering clothes to fit better	reading books to children using a variety of voices
· customers of clothing boutiques · customers of upmarket resale shops · people buying business suits off the rack	· libraries for storytime · daycare centers for storytime or dramatic play · independent publishers who need to get into the audiobook business
teaching people how to cook Ecuadorian food	**painting life size portraits of pets**
· culinary students (high school, trade school, or cooking school) · customers at high end grocery stores · people who subscribe to social outing services (where a bunch of strangers get together and do something for fun each week)	· customers of pet stores · customers of high end pet stores · visitors to dog and kennel shows · visitors to zoos (expand business idea to include not just pets)

Once you have your possible target audience, you can go out into the community and begin conducting your Market Research. You will want to keep in mind these guidelines:

- Contact your target consumer base directly (by phone, email, face to face, or by having them mail you the answers to a questionnaire).

- Look at the information that is already available to you through your local Chamber of Commerce or a similar entity. What data do they have that you can use? Has there been a Consumer Report completed that fits your needs?

- What information is available at the branches of your local library, at the college or university in your area, and through any small business network system?

Notice how each of these guidelines requires you to contact people directly? One of the biggest mistakes people make when they first begin to create their own business is to rely on the internet or an online database for all of their information. That can be one tool, yes, but the best information you will get will come from the actual area that you will be doing business in and from the people who will be paying for your service or your product.

Once you actually begin your company, Market research can still be a valuable tool to keep you making money and to keep your business a success. You will occasionally want to conduct Market Research to make sure that your products are still as effective as you want them to be, that your packaging is meeting the demands of your consumer, that the service you are providing is still valid, meets the clients demands, and competitive on the market for any other product or service that may have come out since you first began your business.

You will also want to get feedback from your clients or your customers on how they find the service or the product that you are offering. You will want to take their comments into consideration because they are the ones who are using the service or the product and can tell you with first hand experience if it is difficult to use if they have an idea for improving it if they have found another use for it, et cetera.

CHAPTER 20:

Being Patient

Winners are patient, and they understand that just as success does not come overnight, neither do profits.

One of the hardest lessons for the owner of a business to learn is that the first profits are not meant for you, but for your business. Do not let a little success go to your head and make all of your hard work up to this point be undone. Remember all of the lessons we have gone through so far about being a Winner, about investing your money wisely, and about being fiscally responsible. Where do your first profits need to go? This is something you need to figure out and plan for **before** you actually see those profits, that way, you have a plan in place and you will stick to the plan when the time comes.

Most businesses reinvest their profits for the first year right back into the business and, if you are still working at another job, this is exactly what you should do as well. If you are not relying on the money for your income, use your profits during the first year to strengthen and grow your business. In this way, you will be guarding against economic downturns, increased costs, and have the ability to grow faster than you would have otherwise.

When your business begins to make money, others will notice, and you may suddenly find yourself with more friends and family members than you remember ever having, and each one will want something: to borrow money, for a loan, for part of the profits, to pitch to you their own business ideas, or anything similar along these lines. You need to have a plan in place, before you ever see any profits, as to how you will react and deal with each request.

You know your friends and family better than anyone. Who are presenting the legitimate offers? Who just wants a hand out or free money? Will that nephew actually work hard and be an asset, or does your sister in law just want an easy job for her son? It is not pessimistic or negative to consider these questions. You need to be a realist when you plan for how others will try to take advantage of your success and your hard work.

When it comes to strangers, decide how you will react as well. Just like having a business plan in place before you actually start your business, you need to have contingency plans in place for any and all situations that may, and will, develop and come to light.

CHAPTER 21

Plan Ahead

Winners plan ahead. As a Winner, how will you plan ahead and protect your business and assets from others?

I am sure that you have seen the headlines and newspaper stories about businesses being sued or taken to court or having made a settlement with a third party. All of these stories have the same source or beginning: someone felt that the business in question had done something wrong towards them, and they were seeking monetary reparations.

Now, many of these instances are legitimate, and the company is at fault: they took safety short cuts that resulted in workers being hurt, they falsified company records so that they would not have to pay employees over time, or some similar illegal measure in which they got caught.

However, some of these stories feature a disgruntled person, either an employee or someone who knows the owner of the company, that sees an easy way to make free money. Those are the people that you have to plan for and guard against, for these are the people that will cost you your hard earned money, put road blocks between you and your goals, and set you attaining your Dream Life backward.

If you are offering a service, you will face different problems than if you are offering a product. (I have written about the product portion next.) When you offer a service, you have direct contact with people and, depending upon the service you offer, their homes and personal property. Now, the majority of people will be up front and honest with you, but you do need to protect yourself against the smaller minority who will see a successful business owner with money and want part of your success.

You need to plan now how you will protect yourself from being sued. When you set up your business, there are paths that you can take right at the beginning to protect yourself and your assets. The most common ways that you can protect yourself, your business, and your assets are:

1. Create a separate entity (corporation, trust, et cetera) that will "own" the business and insulate you and your personal assets from anyone suing the business. You will not be giving up control of your business, or assigning assets to

another person, but, instead, you will be protecting yourself and your personal assets (home, car, savings, et cetera) from anyone who means you harm.

2. Hire a business attorney who will offer guidance, advice, and serve as protection from individuals who mean you or your business harm as well as protect you from things that you do not know (business laws, tax laws, et cetera). When you have an attorney on hand, one who knows you and knows your business, you will be able to met any challenge by another instantly and not be caught unaware, spending time and money interviewing and searching for the right attorney.

3. Watch yourself, your actions, and your words. You are the face and soul of your own business, and anything that you do, say, or share with another reflects back onto your business and company. This includes anything that you do in your personal life, as well as in your online life. If you have a social media page (like Facebook, WeChat, Twitter, Pinterest, or Instagram) and you post something, or allow someone else to post something, on your account that can be construed as offensive, insensitive, or tasteless, this leaves you open for anyone to disapprove, file a claim, or, in some cases, to sue you.

4. Protect your business files and electronic databases. If you are relying on the Internet or an online presence for your business to function, make sure that the connections you use

are secure, that everything you do has been backed up and saved, and that if your system were to go down due to a virus, being hacked, or any other reason, you have a backup system in place where you could still access your files and do the work that you need to do. If you rely on electronic payments from your customers, make sure that their data is always protected, by either not keeping any electronic files on them or having rigid and aggressive protections in place to guard their data and safety.

5. Make sure that one of your first expenditures is for insurance. Just as you would have car insurance to protect yourself and your automobile, house (or renter's) insurance to protect your personal belongings, and health insurance to guard your health and well being, you should have business insurance that protects you, your business, and your business assets from anyone who tries to sue you and your business for any reason.

Winners plan ahead so that they are not caught unaware and assessed fines or fees for failing to fully prepare. They never use the excuse "I did not know" when it comes to the law or rules and regulations.

When starting your own business, we have talked about a lot of the requirements and items you need to plan for. Another important detail is to plan for having employees. When you first begin your own business, you may very well be the only employee you have, and you still need to have certain items and procedures in place.

Some questions to consider are:

- What taxes (city, county, state, and federal) will you be responsible for paying?

- Are you well versed in tax law, or do you need to hire an accountant to handle your taxes? What do you need to know, and what routines and procedures do you need to implement, before you actually begin your own business?

- Do you need to pay into Social Security, Medicare, Worker's Compensation, or any other federal fund? What are the rules and laws in your city, county, and state?

- What insurance requirements do you need? Does this change with an increase in the number of employees?

- Does your city, county, or state have specific laws or regulations that need to be followed?

- Will you need a license, permit, or some other permission from a regulatory body in order to conduct your business?

- Does your city, county, or state have any laws or regulations with regards to health care or offering employee insurance that you have to follow, even if it is just yourself?

- Is there a Better Business Bureau or Small Business Commission or Chamber of Commerce that can help you answer these questions?

CHAPTER 22

Keeping Your Assets Safe

Not everyone is honorable, candid, and honest. The world is full of people who will try to take advantage of you and your success.

When you are ready to begin expanding your business, and you want to include employees other than yourself, how will you address the process? This is a plan that you need to have in place before you begin to hire other people and bring them into your company, your business, and allow them to join all of your hard work.

Some questions to consider are:

- Will you get through a staffing agency and allow them to vet the people first?

- Will you place advertisements in local newspapers, want ads, and on social media?

- Once you have a plan in place, how will you go through the hiring process?

- Will you have a thirty day trial period? Or a sixty day one?

- Will you have an employee handbook that the person will be required to read and sign an agreement saying they agree to abide by the rules and regulations in it? What will be in the handbook?

- How will you handle disciplinary measures? How will you handle firing an employee? What documentation will you need to collect in order to satisfy the rules, regulations, and laws of your city, county, state, and, if applicable, the federal government?

- Do you need to have a nondisclosure agreement for your employees? Do you have business practices that are proprietary or are your products or your services patented, trademarked, or copyrighted and you need to protect them from employees who are fired and may seek retribution or from employees who took the job under false pretenses in order to learn your business model and recreate it for themselves?

- Do you need to have a non compete clause or agreement because you have business practices that are proprietary or are your products or your services patented, trademarked, or copyrighted and you need to protect them from employees who are fired and may seek to begin their own business using your existing customer base or from employees who took the job under false pretenses in order to learn your business model and recreate it for themselves?

Winners and those who are successful must always be aware that there are others who are looking for a shortcut to their own success.

When you began to develop ideas for your business, these ideas fell into two different categories: products and services. The market is full of products and services that are copies or rip offs, of other products and services already on the market.

If you are creating a product for individuals or companies to purchase, you need to ask yourself the following questions in order to make sure that you are protecting your company from the very beginning, before you even have an actual company.

· Do I need a patent for my product? (Is it original?)

· Do I need a trademark for my product or for my business?

· Do I need a copyright?

· Is this a product that could lead to other products? (Similar? Different? Complimentary?) Do I need to patent, trademark, or copyright these ideas, too?

- Is my business attorney able to handle cases of patent violation or trademark infringement?

If you are creating a service for individuals or companies to purchase, you need to ask yourself the following questions in order to make sure that you are protecting your company from the very beginning, before you even have an actual company.

- Do I need a patent for my service? (Is it unique enough?)

- Do I need a trademark for my service or for my business?

- Do I need a copyright?

- Is my business attorney able to handle cases of patent violation or trademark infringement?

- Is this a service that is tied to the area or region that I live in? Could this work in other areas or regions of the state or country? Would I need to change this service in order to be successful in other areas or regions? Do I need to patent, trademark, or copyright these ideas, too?

- Is my service one that could eventually lead to a franchise?

CHAPTER 23

Make a Real Plan

What is your actual plan for starting your own business? Remember that Winners always have a plan for what they do, even if that plan is only for themselves.

We have covered a lot of information, and you have done a lot of thinking and considering. Now is the time to put everything together and create an actual plan for your business.

Take this book and get something to write with (pencil, pen, et cetera) and either sticky notes, paper, and tape, or use your computer and printer. Also, gather all of the lists that you have been writing out for starting your own business.

Now is the time to create your Business Plan. In it, you will finally take all of your ideas and notes and put them down into concrete steps and individual pieces. A Business Plan is a constantly evolving document that you will change again and again based on new data that you find, on a new understanding of your business's needs, and on your own wants and desires.

You will make a Business Plan every time you begin a new business endeavor or adventure. Creating a Business Plan allows you to put everything you have thought of, dreamed, created lists for, and imagined into one solid, concrete document, allowing you to see everything you have already done as well as what you still need to do in order for your business to be a success.

If you are going to bring in outside investors or take out a loan, having a Business Plan shows others that you have carefully thought out each area of your business, done the research, and have concrete ideas on how to begin. It allows you to present your Business Plan to others in a cohesive, coherent fashion that they can see, interpret, and understand. It also allows you to make sure that you have covered every base and avenue before showing it to anyone else.

If you are financing your business on your own, having a Business Plan will allow you to plan everything out and be able to see if you have missed any important steps or failed to plan for any critical business areas. Your Business Plan is like putting your entire business into a single, multiple page goal, where you can see all of the steps that you have taken, as well as the steps that you still need to take.

If you do not know what a Business Plan is, do not worry. I have included step by step directions in this section for you. A Business Plan may sound very official and intimidating but think of it as a report, similar to the one that you wrote when you were in school. That is not over simplifying things, because a Business Plan really is a report about your future business: how will it be structured, have you thought of every contingency, do you have plans in place that will make you and your business a success?

The first part of your Business Plan should be your title page.

- What are you going to call your business? How will you be sure that that name is not already being used by another business? Will you have a website? What will be your web address? Have you already set up a business license, incorporation, or an LLC (limited liability company)?

The second part of your Business Plan should be a lengthy summary of your business.

- What is your actual business? What product or service are you offering? Why is this product or service needed or necessary? How will your business and your workforce be structured?

The third part of your Business Plan should be a description of your business.

· What does the actual business look like? Where is it located? How will it grow over time? What part of the market does it fit into? Where is this part of the market headed in the future?

The fourth part of your Business Plan should be your target audience.

· Who is your target audience? Who is your customer base? Why have you singled out this mart of the market? What did the Market Research that you conducted show? How will you reach these people? How will you keep them coming back to you and your product or service? How will you expand into a wider audience?

The fifth part of your Business Plan should address any competitors and competition that you and your business will face.

· Who, or what, are your current competition or competitors in the area or region? How is your product or service different from what they offer? How can you be sure that there is a large enough customer base to handle both of your companies and your products or services? Why, or how, will your business not create a glut on the market?

The sixth part of your Business Plan should be your product or service plan.

· What is your actual product or service? (This should be a lengthy summary, not a single sentence.) Do I already have a patent, trademark, or copyright for the product or service? (If you do, and you should by this part of the planning process, include the patent number or numbers as well as any trademark and copyright information in this section.) Where will that product or service be produced? How will that product or service be produced? What resources will you need to make this happen? Where will you get those resources from? What is your back up for when your first option is not available? How will your product be packaged, or how will your service be presented? How will your product or service be delivered? How much will this product or service cost to produce? How much will this product or service cost to be delivered to the customer? How much will it sell for? What is your profit margin?

The seventh part of your Business Plan should be how your business operates or functions on a day to day basis.

- Who is in charge? What employees will you need to have? What will be their job responsibilities or roles? What will the daily schedule look like? The weekly schedule? The monthly schedule? How is the business managed, and how does it function?

The eighth part of your Business Plan should be how your business is going to be financed.

- How much will it take to start your business? What are all of the starting costs? (Take into consideration overhead costs, advertising costs, permits, and license costs, payroll, taxes, raw materials, et cetera.) What starting capital do you already have on hand? How much more starting capital do you need? How long can you finance the business without using any of the projected profits?

This is it. This is the end. If you have completed each of the steps in this book, you are now ready to start your own business. If you have not finished each part of this book, then you are still on the right path and have already begun the process. This process may not happen today or tomorrow, but it will happen for you very soon. Remember to keep saying your daily WINNER affirmations, focus on your goals and your Dream Life, get your finances in order, and complete your Business Plan.

Conclusion

Thank you for making it through to the end of *This Book* - I thoroughly enjoyed writing this book and sharing all of my strategies as well as what I have learned over the course of creating my own businesses and pursuing my Dream Life with you. It is my hope that this journey has been informative, clarifying, and has been able to provide you with all of the tools and information you need to define and reach your personal goals, plan, start, and build your own business and achieve your Dream Life.

If you have not already implemented the steps in Part Two: Repeatable Path, then the next step is to do so. Begin with the section on turning your idea into an opportunity, then continue on to financing your Dream Life and follow the steps all the way through to completing your Business Plan.

Please remember that this book and all of the resources in it are always here for you. Do not feel that you have already read this book one time and can now move on. Come back to the lessons and strategies in these pages, refer back to the steps that we have gone through, and, if you find yourself at a crossroads, reread this book.

I wrote this book to be a timeless, step-by-step process, that you can come back to time and again for when you have questions, when you need to rework ideas, for when you are ready to diversify your income streams and sources, or when you are ready to start another new business. Remember that Winners do not have just a single income or revenue stream and are always on the lookout for ways to make more money. The more money you have, the more financial security and safety you have. The more money you have, the closer you are to fulfilling your goals and living your Dream Life.

I encourage you to continue with your daily Winner affirmations and to keep putting items into your daily schedule that show you are actively working on yourself and on your goals. Once you achieve your Dream Life and are spending your time and monetary assets in the ways that you want to, the work does not stop. Do not become complacent but remember two important things: that Winners are always working for themselves and their goals and that the work of a Winner never stops.

When you achieve the goals that you wrote down in Part One: Right Mindset, brainstorm, create and write down new goals that will get you closer and closer to your Dream Life. Never stop striving, learning, earning, and reaching for those goals. When you achieve them, move on to your next set of goals. In doing this, you will achieve your Dream Life and live how you have always envisioned living, doing what you have always wanted to do, and spending your time and your money on the things that matter the most to you.

Remember what I told you at the very start of our journey together: by reading the advice, messages, and instructions in *This Book* and following the lessons and information I have presented in it, you are taking ownership of your life, leaving the dream state of "if I only won the lottery," and living in a reality where you are in control, where you are in charge, and where you will be successful. You are there.

I wrote this book for you, for you to be able to refer back to again and again, and I want you to know that I am here for you, that I believe in you, and I know that you will be a success. You are a Winner already, and you will continue to show and prove that to yourself and to the world. When you have finished building your own business and are living your Dream Life, I will be there congratulating you on all of your hard work!

I am also writing a second book, the title is still to be chosen, and the lessons in it are a continuation of what you have read here, taking you further on your journey of being a Winner and achieving your Dream Life. If you have found the ideas and strategies in *This Book* to be helpful, I know that you will be equally pleased with the new steps and information in my next book so, stay tuned.

Finally, if you found this book helpful and useful in any way, a positive review on Amazon is always deeply appreciated!

Now, go out and show the world the Winner that you are! Be positive, be deliberate, be ready to take charge of yourself and your life, and go live your Dream Life!

Thank you,